101 *Quick & Easy* 30 MINUTE RECIPES -for- DIABETICS

Dr. A. Francis

December | 2022

Copyright © 2022 T.C.PASK

All rights reserved

No part of this publication may be reproduced, distributed, or transmitted in any form or by any means, including photocopying, recording, or other electronic or mechanical methods, without the prior written permission of the publisher, except in the case of brief quotations embodied in critical reviews and certain other noncommercial uses permitted by copyright law.

ISBN 979-8-9873520-1-4

t.c.paskpublishing@gmail.com

LUNCHES

DINNERS

BONUS RECIPES

BREAKFASTS

AIR FRYER MEALS

ASIAN LETTUCE *Wraps*

INGREDIENTS

For 4 servings

- 1 lb cooked chicken breast, *shredded*
- 1 cup shredded cabbage
- Large lettuce leaves
- 2 scallions, *thinly sliced*
- 6 tsp peanut sauce

HOW TO MAKE

- Spoon chicken, cabbage into lettuce leaves. Add scallions.
- Drizzle with peanut sauce.

Dinner

TURKEY & CHICKPEA *Stew*

INGREDIENTS

For 4 servings

- 1 tbsp olive oil
- 1 lb lean ground turkey
- 2 cans chickpeas, *drained*
- 1 medium onion, *chopped*
- 2 medium carrots, *diced*
- 4 cloves garlic, *minced*
- 3 tbsp tomato paste
- 4 cups chicken broth
- 3 cups spinach

HOW TO MAKE

- Mash 1 can chickpeas.
- Heat oil in a large pot over medium-high heat. Add turkey, onion, carrots, garlic, cook 3 mins.
- Add tomato paste, broth, salt, mashed and whole chickpeas.
- Cover and bring to a simmer (about 10 mins).
- Add spinach, cook 2 mins.

VEG HUMMUS *Sandwiches*

INGREDIENTS

For 4 servings

- 1 cup cucumber, *sliced*
- 8 slices whole-grain bread
- 1 medium bell pepper, *sliced*
- 2 cups mixed salad greens
- 12 tbsp beetroot hummus
- 1 cup carrot, *shredded*
- 1 avocado, *mashed*

HOW TO MAKE

- Spread one slice of bread with avocado, the other with hummus. Top with veggies.
- Slice in half and serve.

Dinner

One-Pot SHRIMP & BROCCOLI

INGREDIENTS

For 4 servings

- 1 lb shrimp, *peeled*
- 4 cups broccoli florets
- ½ cup bell pepper, *diced*
- 6 cloves garlic, *sliced*
- 2 tsp lemon juice
- 3 tbsp olive oil

HOW TO MAKE

- Heat 2 tbsp oil in a saucepan over medium heat. Add garlic, cook about 1 min. Add bell pepper, broccoli, salt, pepper. Cover and cook 5 mins. Transfer to a bowl.
- Add 1 tbsp oil to the pot. Add shrimp, cook 5 mins. Return the broccoli mixture to the pot, add lemon juice and stir to combine.

CHICKPEA *Wraps*

Lunch

INGREDIENTS

For 4 servings

- 1 tsp sugar free hot sauce
- 2 cans chickpeas, *drained*
- ½ cup cucumber sticks
- 2 cups romaine lettuce
- 1 cup carrot, *shredded*
- 4 whole-wheat wraps
- ¾ cup greek yogurt

HOW TO MAKE

- Roast the chickpeas 20 mins.
- Combine yogurt and hot sauce.
- Divide all ingredients among wraps. Roll up. Cut in half.

Dinner

SWEET POTATO *Enchiladas*

INGREDIENTS

For 4 servings

- ¾ cup pinto beans, *rinsed*
- 1 cup yellow onion, *sliced*
- ½ cup low carb enchilada sauce
- 3 tbsp reduced-fat cheese
- 1 sweet potato, *peeled and cut into cubes*
- 1 tbsp olive oil
- 12 egg wraps

HOW TO MAKE

- Microwave sweet potato with water about 5 mins. Drain.
- Heat oil in a medium skillet. Add onion, beans, sweet potato, cook 2 mins. Stir in sauce.
- Spoon 3 tbsp of potato mixture into egg wrap. Fold the wrap. Repeat with all wraps.
- Broil 3 mins. Sprinkle cheese over wraps.

VEGGIE PASTA *Salad*

INGREDIENTS

For 4 servings

- 6 oz whole-wheat pasta
- 8 oz cherry tomatoes, halved
- ¾ cup reduced-fat feta cheese
- 1 medium zucchini, *chopped*
- 1 cup broccoli, *chopped*
- 2 tsp olive oil

HOW TO MAKE

- Heat oil in skillet. Add broccoli, zucchini, tomatoes. Cook 5 mins.
- Cook pasta. Mix vegetables with pasta. Toss in feta cheese.

TERIYAKI CHICKEN *Quinoa Bowl*

INGREDIENTS

For 4 servings

- 2 cups cooked quinoa
- 2 medium chicken breasts
- 4 tbsp apple cider vinegar
- 3 tsp Monk fruit sweetener
- 4 tbsp coconut aminos
- 1 cup green beans
- 1 tsp garlic powder
- 2 tsp ground ginger
- 4 tsp almond flour

HOW TO MAKE

- Preheat 1 tbsp oil in a skillet. Add chicken. Cook 10 mins.
- Whisk together coconut aminos, sweetener, ginger, garlic powder, almond flour, vinegar to make sauce.
- Add green beans to chicken. Pour sauce and simmer until chicken is fully cooked.
- Serve with cooked quinoa.

TUNA SALAD *Wraps*

INGREDIENTS

For 4 servings

- 1 stalk celery, *diced*
- 4 whole-wheat wraps
- 4 cans (4 oz) tuna, *drained*
- 1 cup greek yogurt
- 1 red bell pepper
- 1 cup spinach

HOW TO MAKE

- Drain tuna. Add yogurt, bell pepper, celery to the tuna. Mix.
- Divide mixture, spinach among wraps. Roll up. Cut in half.

ALASKA HALIBUT *with Quinoa*

INGREDIENTS

For 4 servings

- 3 tbsp olive oil
- 2 tbsp lemon juice
- 1 tbsp parsley, *minced*
- 1 tsp garlic, *minced*
- ¼ tsp black pepper
- 4 four-ounce halibut fillets
- 2 cups quinoa
- ¼ cup spinach

HOW TO MAKE

- Preheat oven to 400°F.
- In a baking dish, add halibut skin side down, drizzle with oil.
- Top with parsley, garlic, lemon juice. Season with salt and pepper.
- Bake for 15 mins. Drizzle with lemon juice, serve with cooked quinoa and spinach.

SHRIMP & BEAN *Salad*

INGREDIENTS

For 4 servings

- 1 lb cooked shrimp
- 1 can (15 oz) black beans
- 1 red bell pepper, *chopped*
- 1 cucumber, chopped
- ½ cup fresh cilantro
- 2 tbsp olive oil
- 1 tbsp fresh lime juice

HOW TO MAKE

- In a large bowl combine all ingredients, add salt to taste, mix well, toss until the shrimp are well coated.

Tilapia AND ZUCCHINI NOODLES

INGREDIENTS

For 4 servings

- 2 large zucchini
- ½ tsp ground cumin
- ½ tsp smoked paprika
- 4 tilapia fillets (6 oz each)
- 2 garlic cloves, minced
- ¼ tsp garlic powder
- 1 cup pico de gallo
- ½ tsp pepper
- 2 tsp olive oil

HOW TO MAKE

- Using a spiralizer, cut zucchini into thin strands.
- Mix all spices and salt to taste, sprinkle onto tilapia.
- In a large skillet, heat oil over medium-high heat. Cook tilapia until fish begins to flake easily with a fork. Remove from skillet.
- Cook zucchini with garlic, about 2 mins. Serve with pico de gallo.

CHICKEN & EGG *Salad*

INGREDIENTS

For 4 servings

- 4 chicken breasts
- 2 tbsp fat-free mayo
- 1 tbsp curry powder
- 4 hard-boiled eggs
- 1 cup avocado, *cubes*

HOW TO MAKE

- Bake chicken at 365°F for 20 mins.
- Cut chicken and eggs. Combine everything in a bowl, add salt to taste.

Dinner

TURKEY CABBAGE *Stew*

INGREDIENTS

For 4 servings

- 1 lb ground turkey
- 1 can diced tomatoes
- 1 medium onion, *chopped*
- 3 garlic cloves, *minced*
- 3 cups cabbage, *chopped*
- 2 medium carrots, *sliced*
- 1 tsp dried oregano
- ¼ tsp dried thyme
- ¾ cup water

HOW TO MAKE

- Cook the turkey, onion, and garlic in a large saucepan over medium heat until meat is no longer pink.
- Stir in remaining ingredients.
- Let simmer 10 mins (until vegetables are tender).

TUNA NICOISE *Salad*

INGREDIENTS

For 4 servings

- 1½ cup arugula
- ⅓ cup light Italian salad dressing
- 4 boiled eggs, *quartered*
- ¼ cup olives
- 1 can (10 oz) tuna, *drained*
- 2 cups grape tomatoes

HOW TO MAKE

- In a large bowl, add arugula and dressing, toss well to combine.
- Arrange on a platter. Top with the eggs, olives, tuna, tomatoes.

Mushroom SMOTHERED CHICKEN

INGREDIENTS

For 4 servings

- 1 tsp olive oil
- ¾ cups sliced mushrooms
- 3 green onions, sliced
- 2 cups fresh baby spinach
- 4 tbsp chopped pecans
- 4 chicken breast halves
- 2 slices reduced-fat provolone cheese, *halved*

HOW TO MAKE

- In a large skillet, heat oil, saute mushrooms and green onions until tender. Stir in spinach and pecans until spinach is wilted. Remove from heat.
- Preheat oven to 425°F. Sprinkle chicken with salt. Bake for 20 mins.
- Top with cheese and mushroom mixture.

EASY SALMON *Wraps*

INGREDIENTS

For 4 servings

- 8 oz. smoked salmon
- 8 tsp low fat cream cheese
- ½ cup red onion, *thinly sliced*
- 4 8-inch whole grain tortillas
- 2 tsp fresh or dried basil
- 1 cup arugula

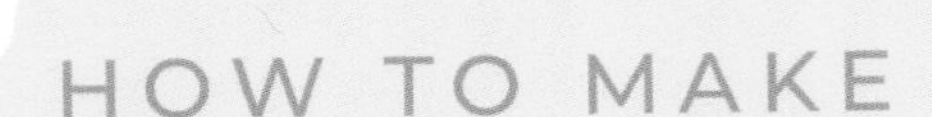

HOW TO MAKE

- Warm tortillas in the oven.
- Mix together the cream cheese, basil, spread it onto the tortillas.
- Top it off with salmon, onion, arugula. Roll up and serve.

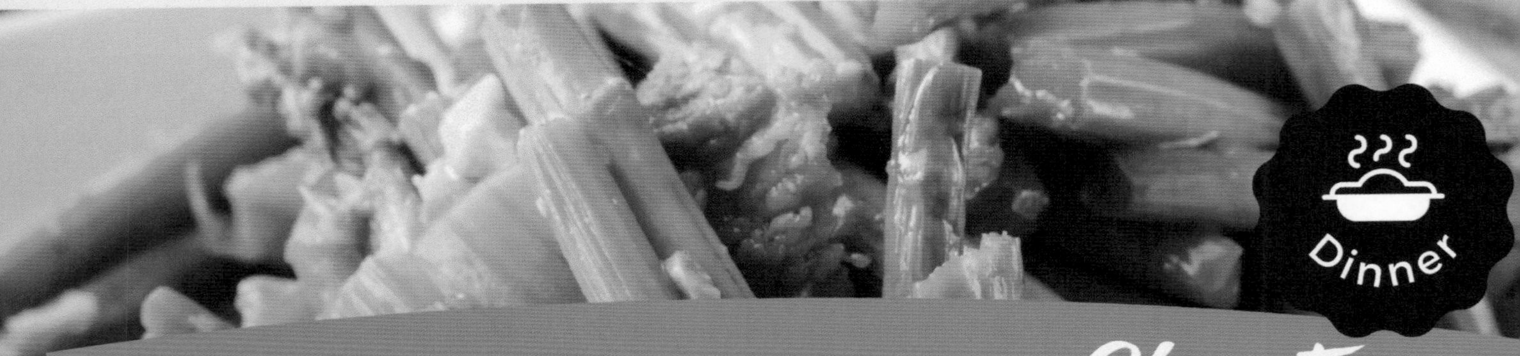

Dinner

ASPARAGUS & TURKEY *Stir-Fry*

INGREDIENTS

For 4 servings

- 1 lb ground turkey
- 1 lb frozen cut asparagus
- 1 cup carrots, *shredded*
- 4 green onions, *sliced*
- 2 cloves garlic, *minced*
- ¼ cup coconut aminos
- ¼ cup sweet chilli sauce, *sugar free*
- ¼ cup fresh basil, *sliced*

HOW TO MAKE

- Cook ground turkey in a large skillet over medium heat, until turkey is browned.
- Stir in carrots, garlic, green onions, asparagus, cook 2 mins.
- Stir in chili sauce, basil and coconut aminos, cook 3 mins.

Savory OATMEAL

INGREDIENTS

For 4 servings

- 4 cups vegetable broth
- 12 large sun-dried tomato
- 12 tbsp fat-free greek yogurt
- 4 tsp fresh cilantro, *sliced*
- 4 tbsp goat cheese, *crumbled*
- ¼ tsp turmeric powder
- 2 cups rolled oats

HOW TO MAKE

- Bring the broth, tomatoes to boil.
- Stir in the oats, reduce heat to medium. Cook 5 mins, stirring. Stir in yogurt. Serve with cilantro and cheese.

SALMON QUINOA Risotto

INGREDIENTS

For 4 servings

- 1 medium yellow onion, *diced*
- 2 cups vegetable broth
- 4 cups almond milk
- 4 tsp italian herbs
- 4 salmon fillets
- 2 cups cooked quinoa
- 2 tsp olive oil

HOW TO MAKE

- Heat up olive oil in a skillet. Add onion, sauté for 2 mins.
- Add quinoa, almond milk, vegetable broth and Italian herbs. Cook 20 mins, stirring.
- Heat up a skillet. Add salmon fillets, let sear for 3 mins on each side. Season with salt.
- Serve salmon with quinoa and your favorite vegetables.

TUNA CHICKPEA *Pita*

INGREDIENTS

For 4 servings

- 2 whole wheat pita
- 2 cans (10 oz) tuna, *drained*
- ½ cup *fat-free* greek yogurt
- 1 can (15 oz) chickpeas, *drained*
- ¼ cup fresh parsley
- 2 tbsp lemon juice
- 1 cup lettuce

HOW TO MAKE

- To a medium mixing bowl, add tuna, chickpeas, lettuce. Pour the greek yogurt, lemon juice, parsley.
- Slice pita pockets in half. Add tuna salad mixture.

TURKEY & ZUCCHINI *Curry*

INGREDIENTS

For 4 servings

- 2 tbsp olive oil
- 2 shallots, *thinly sliced*
- 1 cup zucchini, *chopped*
- 1 tbsp ginger, *minced*
- 1½ tbsp curry powder
- 2 cups baby spinach
- 1 lb lean ground turkey
- 1 can light coconut milk
- 1 tbsp tamari

HOW TO MAKE

- Preheat large saucepan over medium high heat. Add shallots and sauté for 4-5 mins. Add garlic, ginger, curry powder, salt, cook for 3 mins. Add turkey, cook for 10 mins. Add coconut milk, tamari, zucchini, spinach. Cover and simmer for 10 mins.

TURKEY COBB *Salad*

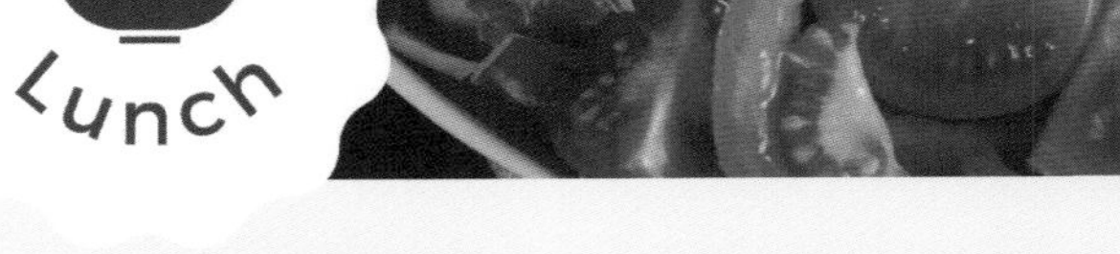

INGREDIENTS

For 4 servings

- 4 boiled eggs, *peeled*
- 1½ cup cherry tomatoes
- 1 cup cooked turkey, *shredded*
- 5 cups lettuce, *chopped*
- ½ cup feta cheese, *reduced fat*
- ½ cup red onion, *chopped*
- 4 tbsp ranch dressing

HOW TO MAKE

- Divide lettuce between 4 bowls. Starting with eggs, arrange the remaining ingredients in rows on the lettuce.
- Drizzle 2 tbsp of ranch dressing.

SALMON & ASPARAGUS *Bake*

INGREDIENTS

For 4 servings

- 1 onion, *thinly sliced*
- 4 (4-oz) salmon fillets
- ½ cup cherry tomatoes
- 1 lb asparagus
- ¼ cup dijon mustard
- 1 tbsp cup olive oil
- 3 tsp Monk fruit sweetener

HOW TO MAKE

- Place onion and tomatoes in the middle of the baking sheet. Place the salmon fillets on top and place the asparagus around.
- In a small bowl, whisk together mustard, olive oil, sweetener. Spread mixture on top of the salmon fillets.
- Preheat oven to 400°F. Bake 20 mins.

SWEET POTATO *Soup*

INGREDIENTS

For 4 servings

- 1 tbsp olive oil
- 1 onion, *roughly chopped*
- 2 large carrots, *roughly chopped*
- 1½ in ginger, *finely chopped*
- 10 oz sweet potatoes
- 2 cups vegetable stock

HOW TO MAKE

- Heat the oil in a saucepan. Add the onion, carrots, ginger, fry for 5 mins. Add sweet potatoes, stock
- Simmer with the lid on for 15 mins. Blend the soup.

CHICKEN BROWN RICE *Pasta*

INGREDIENTS

For 4 servings

- 1 lb chicken breast
- 1 cup mushrooms, *sliced*
- 1 cup cherry tomatoes
- 1 large zucchini, *chopped*
- 3 tbsp basil leaves
- 2 cups brown rice pasta, *uncooked*
- 2 tbsp tamari
- ½ cup fat-free greek yogurt

HOW TO MAKE

- Bring a pot of water to the boil, add pasta. Cook until al dente.
- Heat up olive oil in a skillet. Add chicken, mushrooms, zucchini.
- When the chicken is cooked through, add halved tomatoes, tamari and heat through.
- Take the heat off, add the pasta, greek yogurt and stir to combine.
- Season with fresh basil leaves.

RED LENTIL *Soup*

INGREDIENTS

For 4 servings

- 1 tsp cumin seeds
- 1 tbsp olive oil
- 1 red onion, *chopped*
- 1 cup red lentils
- 4 cups vegetable stock
- 1 can tomatoes
- 1 can chickpeas

HOW TO MAKE

- Heat a large saucepan, add olive oil, cumin, onion, saute for 5 mins. Add lentils, stock, tomatoes, chickpeas, salt to taste. Simmer for 20 mins.
- Blend the soup

LEMON TILAPIA *with Mushrooms*

INGREDIENTS

For 4 servings

- 2 tbsp olive oil
- ½ lb mushrooms, *sliced*
- ¾ tsp lemon-pepper seasoning
- 3 garlic cloves, *minced*
- 4 (6 oz) tilapia fillets
- ⅛ tsp cayenne pepper
- 1 tomato, *chopped*
- 3 green onions, *sliced*

HOW TO MAKE

- In a skillet, heat oil medium heat. Add mushrooms, ¼ tsp lemon-pepper seasoning, cook and stir 3-5 mins. Add garlic, cook 30 seconds longer.
- Place fillets over mushrooms, sprinkle with cayenne and remaining lemon pepper. Cook, covered, 7 mins. Top with tomato and green onions.

EDAMAME *Stir-Fry*

Lunch

INGREDIENTS

For 4 servings

- 14 oz shelled edamame
- 1 cup cauliflower, *chopped*
- 1 cup bell peppers, *diced*
- 4 cloves garlic, *chopped*
- 1 cup broccoli, *chopped*
- 1 cup green beans
- 2 tsp olive oil

HOW TO MAKE

- Heat oil in a pan. Sauté garlic a min. Add cauliflower, bell peppers, salt, edamame, broccoli, beans. Cover, cook until the vegetables are softened.

Dinner

CHICKEN CAULIFLOWER *"Rice"*

INGREDIENTS

For 4 servings

- 1 large head cauliflower
- 1 lb chicken breasts
- ½ tsp pepper
- 1 tbsp olive oil
- 1 bell pepper, *chopped*
- 1 small onion, *chopped*
- 1 garlic clove, *minced*
- ½ cup tomato juice
- ¼ cup cilantro, *chopped*

HOW TO MAKE

- Cut and pulse cauliflower in a food processor until it resembles rice.
- In a large skillet, saute chicken (cut into cubes) with salt to taste and pepper about 5 mins. Add bell pepper, onion and garlic, cook 3 mins. Stir in tomato juice. Add cauliflower. Cover, cook 7 mins. Add cilantro.

CRAB *Cakes*

INGREDIENTS

For 4 servings

- 1 lb lump crabmeat
- 4 small shallots, *diced*
- 4 tbsp green onions, *chopped*
- 4 tbsp fat-free greek yogurt
- 1 cup almond flour
- 2 tbsp olive oil, *for frying*
- 2 large eggs

HOW TO MAKE

- In a mixing bowl, add all of the ingredients and mix
- Form patties. In a pan add the olive oil. Fry patties for 5 mins per side.
- Serve with your favorite vegetables.

SALMON BROWN RICE *Bowl*

INGREDIENTS

For 4 servings

- 1 cup brown rice
- 1 salmon fillet, *cubes*
- ½ cup fat-free greek yogurt
- 2 tbsp sriracha hot sauce
- ⅓ cup coconut aminos
- 3 small avocados, *sliced*
- 2 cups cucumber, *sliced*
- 6 radishes, *thinly sliced*
- 2 tbsp sesame seeds

HOW TO MAKE

- Cook brown rice.
- Heat up olive oil (2 tsp) in a skillet. Cook salmon with salt and pepper for 8 mins.
- In a bowl, whisk yogurt, sriracha and coconut aminos.
- Divide rice among 4 bowls. Top with salmon, avocado, radish, cucumber. Drizzle sauce. Sprinkle with sesame seeds

LENTIL TOMATO *Salad*

INGREDIENTS

For 4 servings

- ¼ cup balsamic vinegar
- 1 ½ cups cherry tomatoes
- 1 can (15 oz) lentils, *drained*
- 1 red onion, *thinly sliced*
- 1 cup baby spinach, *chopped*
- ¼ cup cilantro, *chopped*

HOW TO MAKE

- Halve cherry tomatoes.
- Add all ingredients to a bowl and toss to combine. Add salt to taste and adjust vinegar.

One-Skillet CHICKEN & FARRO

INGREDIENTS

For 4 servings

- 1 lb chicken breast, *cubed*
- 1 cup onion, *diced*
- 2 cans chicken broth
- 2 cups farro
- 1 (14.5 ounce) can Italian-style diced tomatoes
- 1 cup baby spinach
- 1 tsp dried parsley
- 1 tsp basil

HOW TO MAKE

- Heat a skillet over medium heat. Cook chicken and onion 5 mins. Remove chicken.
- Pour chicken broth into skillet and bring to a boil. Stir in farro. Cover, reduce heat, cook 15 mins. Return chicken to skillet. Stir in tomatoes, spinach, basil, and parsley. Season with salt and pepper to taste. Simmer 5 mins.

ZUCCHINI *Muffins*

INGREDIENTS

For 4 servings

- 3 eggs
- 1 cup wholemeal flour
- 2 cups zucchini, *grated*
- ½ cup low fat cheese, *grated*
- 1 can corn kernels, *drained*
- 1 can kidney beans, *drained*
- ¼ cup olive oil

HOW TO MAKE

- Preheat oven to 360°F.
- Whisk eggs and flour together. Add all remain ingredients. Mix.
- Divide mixture among muffin cups. Bake for 20 mins.

Dinner

Creamy DIJON CHICKEN

INGREDIENTS

For 4 servings

- ½ cup *nonfat* half-and-half cream
- ¼ cup dijon mustard
- 4 chicken breast halves
- 2 tsp olive oil
- 1 onion, *thinly sliced*
- 1 tsp dried thyme

HOW TO MAKE

- Whisk together cream and mustard. Sprinkle chicken with salt and pepper to taste.
- Heat oil in a large skillet. Brown chicken on both sides. Reduce heat to medium. Add onion and cream mixture, bring to a boil. Reduce heat and cook 10 mins. Sprinkle with thyme.

BROCCOLI *Fritters*

INGREDIENTS

For 4 servings

- 1 lb broccoli rice
- 10 oz hummus
- 2 small eggs
- ⅔ cup wholemeal breadcrumbs
- ½ tsp garlic powder
- ⅓ tsp salt

HOW TO MAKE

- Thoroughly combine broccoli rice, hummus, eggs, crumbs, salt, garlic powder. Shape into fritters.
- Fry the fritters 7 mins per side.

Creamy LENTIL CURRY

INGREDIENTS

For 4 servings

- 1 cup red lentils
- 1 (28 oz) can diced fire-roasted tomatoes
- 1 (13.5 oz) can light coconut milk
- 1 tbsp curry powder
- 1 (13.5 oz) can chickpeas, drained
- 1 cup spinach

HOW TO MAKE

- Add red lentils, coconut milk, tomatoes, curry powder, salt to taste to a saucepan. Bring to a simmer of medium-high heat for 10 mins.
- Stir in spinach and chickpeas. Simmer for 10 mins. Add salt to taste.
- Serve alone or spooned over brown rice.

KALE & QUINOA *Salad*

INGREDIENTS

For 4 servings

Lunch

- 2 tbsp olive oil
- 1 cup quinoa
- 1 cup kale, *roughly chopped*
- 1 cup sun-dried tomatoes
- 1 can chickpeas, *drained*
- ⅓ cup walnuts, *chopped*
- 1 tbsp lemon juice

HOW TO MAKE

- Cook quinoa according to instructions on package.
- Massage the kale. Combine all ingredient, add salt to taste. Drizzle with oil, mix once more.

Dinner

VEGGIE & TOFU *Stir-Fry*

INGREDIENTS

For 4 servings

- 18 oz extra-firm tofu
- 2 cups broccoli, *chopped*
- 1 carrot, *sliced into sticks*
- 1 tsp fresh ginger, *minced*
- 2 tbsp apple cider vinegar
  2 tbsp tahini
- 1 tsp sriracha
- ¼ cup tamari
- 1 tbsp olive oil

HOW TO MAKE

- Add oil, tofu (cut into cubes) to a skillet and cook for about 2 mins, set aside.
- Mix together sriracha, vinegar, tahini, tamari.
- Add vegetables with ¼ cup of water, cover and cook 5 mins.
- Add tofu to the veggies. Pour the sauce and cook 2 mins.

BUCKWHEAT *Bowl*

INGREDIENTS

For 4 servings

- 1 cup buckwheat groats
- 1 cup edamame, *shelled*
- 1 sheet nori, *cut into thin strips*
- 2 tbsp sesame seeds, *toasted*
- 1 avocado, *sliced*
- 2 tbsp sriracha
- 1 cup kimchi

HOW TO MAKE

- Cook buckwheat according to instructions on package.
- Divide buckwheat among 4 bowls. Add edamame and avocado. Drizzl with sriracha, top with kimchi, nori

One Pot CHICKPEA & QUINOA

INGREDIENTS

For 4 servings

- 1 tbsp olive oil
- 2 garlic cloves, *minced*
- ½ tsp dried thyme
- 1½ cup quinoa
- 1 cup green olives, *sliced*
- ½ cup sun dried tomatoes, *chopped*
- 1 cup spinach, *chopped*
- 1 can chickpeas, *drained*

HOW TO MAKE

- Cook quinoa according to instructions on package.
- Heat oil in a saucepan over medium heat. Add thyme, garlic, sauté 2 mins.
- Add quinoa, olives, tomatoes. Cook 15 seconds. Stir in spinach and chickpeas. Let sit for a 1 min. Season with salt and pepper to taste.

QUINOA *Bake*

INGREDIENTS

For 4 servings

- 1 cup quinoa
- ½ cup low fat cheese, *grated*
- 2 cups baby spinach
- ½ cup almond milk
- 1 large egg
- 1 olive oil

HOW TO MAKE

- Cook quinoa according to instructions on package.
- Whisk milk, egg, salt in a bowl.
- Add mixture, spinach, cheese to quinoa, stir. Bake 15 mins at 375°F.

Dinner

BUNLESS SALMON *Burgers*

INGREDIENTS

For 4 servings

- 1 lb salmon fillet
- 1 cup wholemeal breadcrumbs
- 2 eggs
- ¼ cup fat-free greek yogurt
- 1 tbsp lemon juice
- 1 tsp mustard
- 2 cups lettuce
- 1 tsp olive oil

HOW TO MAKE

- Chop the salmon fillet into small pieces and transfer it into a bowl, add salt to taste.
- Stir in the rest of ingredients.
- Heat a little oil in a large non-stick grill pan over medium heat. Divide the mixture into 4 and form neat patties. Fry the patties 4 mins on each side. Serve with lettuce.

CHICKEN SLAW *Tacos*

INGREDIENTS

For 4 servings

- 1 tbsp cider vinegar
- ⅓ cup fat-free greek yogurt
- 2 cups red cabbage, *shredded*
- 2 cups cooked chicken breast, *shredded*
- 3 tbsp light barbecue sauce
- 8 corn tortillas

HOW TO MAKE

- Combine yogurt, vinegar, salt in a large bowl. Add cabbage, toss.
- Combine chicken, barbecue sauce.
- Heat tortillas. Fill each tortilla with chicken and slaw.

Dinner

CHICKEN VEGGIE *Stir-Fry*

INGREDIENTS

For 4 servings

- 2 tbsp coconut aminos
- ¾ cup chicken broth
- 2 ½ cups broccoli, *chopped*
- 1 lb chicken breasts
- 2 tbsp olive oil
- 1 ½ cups carrots, *sliced*
- 1 small yellow onion
- 1 bell pepper, *sliced*
- 1 cup peas

HOW TO MAKE

- Heat oil in a skillet over medium-high heat. Add chicken (cut into pieces). Cook 6 mins.
- Add in carrots, onions, broccoli, bell pepper, peas, saute 10 mins. Pour coconut aminos and chicken broth, saute for another 1-2 mins. tossing constantly.

BUCKWHEAT *Salad*

Lunch

INGREDIENTS

For 4 servings

- 1 cup buckwheat groats
- ½ cup red onion, *diced*
- 2 cups cherry tomatoes
- 1 cup pitted kalamata olives
- 1 cup baby spinach
- 2 bell peppers, sliced
- 2 tbsp olive oil

HOW TO MAKE

- Cook buckwheat according to instructions on package.
- Combine cooled groats with tomato, spinach, olives, and bell pepper in a salad bowl. Add olive oil, salt to taste.

CREAMY TUNA & PASTA *Bake*

INGREDIENTS

For 4 servings

- 14 oz wholemeal pasta
- 1 can (12 oz) tuna, *drained*
- 1 cup spinach
- 1 can corn kernels, *drained*
- ½ cup wholemeal breadcrumbs
- 1 cup tomato sauce
- ⅓ cup reduced fat mozzarella cheese, *grated*

HOW TO MAKE

- Warm the oven to 350°F .
- Cook the pasta “al dente”.
- Add the spinach for 1 min and allow to wilt.
- Drain and transfer to a baking dish. Mix in the tuna, corn and tomato sauce
- Top with mozzarella and breadcrumbs.
- Bake for 15 mins.

WHITE BEAN *Patties*

Lunch

INGREDIENTS

For 4 servings

- 2 tbsp olive oil
- 1 can (15 oz) white beans
- 4 slices wholemeal bread
- 2 tbsp nutritional yeast
- ½ tsp onion powder
- ½ tsp garlic salt
- ½ tsp of cumin

HOW TO MAKE

- In a food processor, place all ingredients and process until well incorporated. Form patties.
- Heat oil in a skillet. Cook patties until lightly brown each side.

Dinner

SPICY LENTIL *Stew*

INGREDIENTS

For 4 servings

- 1 tbsp olive oil
- 1 large carrot, *diced*
- 2 celery sticks, *diced*
- 2 sweet potatoes, *diced*
- 1 garlic clove, *crushed*
- 3 tomatoes, *chopped*
- 2 ½ cups vegetable stock
- 4 tbsp fat-free greek yogurt
- 1 cup red lentils

HOW TO MAKE

- Heat the oil in a saucepan over a medium-high heat. Add the carrot, celery, garlic and potatoes, cook 5 mins.
- Stir in the tomatoes and lentils. Add the vegetable stock, salt to taste and simmer for 20 mins.
- Serve with yogurt.

Thai CAULIFLOWER

Lunch

INGREDIENTS

For 4 servings

- 1 big head cauliflower, *cut into florets*
- 2 tsp thai red curry paste
- ½ cup light coconut milk
- 1 can chickpeas, *drained*
- 1 tbsp olive oil

HOW TO MAKE

- Heat oven to 400°F. Bake (20 mins) chickpeas and cauliflower with oil.
- Combine curry paste with milk in a saucepan. Simmer 2 mins. Pour it over cauliflower and chickpeas.

Dinner

Turkey STUFFED SWEET POTATO

INGREDIENTS

For 4 servings

- 1 green onion, *chopped*
- 4 medium sweet potatoes
- 1 lb ground turkey
- 1 can (9 oz) black beans, *drained*
- 1 cup corn kernels
- 1 tbsp taco seasoning
- ¼ cup fat-free greek yogurt
- 1 tbsp olive oil

HOW TO MAKE

- Wash potatoes thoroughly, pierce with a fork. Microwave 5 min, turning halfway.
- Cut potatoes in half and fluff their centers with a fork.
- Heat the oil in a large skillet. Add turkey, cook 10 mins. Add beans, corn, taco seasoning and mix. Spoon mixture into sweet potato, serve with yogurt.

Baked TEMPEH

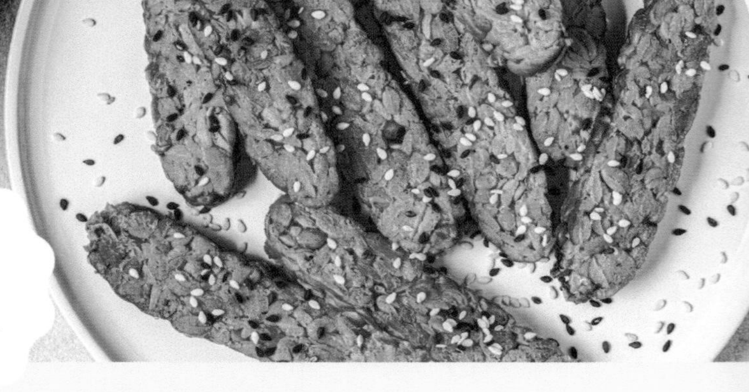

INGREDIENTS

For 4 servings

- 16 oz block tempeh
- 2 tbsp tamari
- 2 tbsp nutritional yeast
- 1 tbsp sesame seeds
- 2 cups raw vegetables, *to serve*

HOW TO MAKE

- Cut the tempeh into cubes. Drizzle the tamari, then stir well. Sprinkle the nutritional yeast and mix again.
- Preheat the oven to 400°F.
- Bake 20 mins. Serve with veggies.

Dinner

QUINOA & SHRIMP *Stir Fry*

INGREDIENTS

For 4 servings

- 2 tbsp olive oil
- 1 onion, *finely chopped*
- 1 clove garlic minced
- ½ tsp chili powder
- 2 cups dry quinoa
- 1 lb shrimp, *peeled*
- ½ tsp chili powder
- ½ cup parsley, *chopped*
- Juice of one lemon

HOW TO MAKE

- Cook quinoa according to instructions on package.
- Heat the olive oil in a skillet. Add the onion, garlic, cook 3 mins. Add the shrimp, chili powder, salt. Sauté until no longer translucent.
- Mix the quinoa and shrimp, drizzle with lemon juice, sprinkle with parsley.

CAULIFLOWER *Muffins*

INGREDIENTS

For 4 servings

- 4 cups cauliflower rice
- ½ cup onion, *diced*
- 1½ cups low fat cheese, *shredded*
- 1 tsp Italian seasoning
- 2 eggs

HOW TO MAKE

- Preheat oven to 350°F.
- Mix all ingredients in a large bowl. Scoop mixture into muffin cups.
- Bake for 25 mins or until firm and starting to brown.

Almond CRUSTED FISH

INGREDIENTS

For 4 servings

- 1 egg
- 1 lb fish fillets
- ½ cup sliced almonds
- 1 cup wholemeal breadcrumbs
- 3 tbsp almond milk
- ¼ tsp chili powder
- 2 tbsp olive oil

HOW TO MAKE

- Prepare one bowl with egg and milk, and one bowl with breadcrumbs, chopped almonds, salt. Dip each fillet, one at a time into egg mixture then into almond mixture.
- Preheat oven to 450 °F. Bake in oven with oil for 6 mins per side, flipping halfway.

BLACK BEAN *Soup*

Lunch

INGREDIENTS

For 4 servings

- 1 tbsp olive oil
- 1 medium onion, *chopped*
- 1 tsp ground cumin
- 2 cloves garlic
- 2 cans (14 oz) black beans
- 2 cups vegetable broth
- ½ cup avocado, *cubes*

HOW TO MAKE

- Saute onion in olive oil. Add cumin, garlic and cook 30 seconds. Add black beans and vegetable broth. Bring to a simmer. Blend the ingredients. Serve with avocado.

Dinner

Spicy COCONUT SHRIMP

INGREDIENTS

For 4 servings

- 2 tbsp olive oil
- 1 cup onion, *chopped*
- 1 tbsp garlic, *minced*
- 2 tsp ginger, *minced*
- ⅛ tsp turmeric
- 1 cup canned tomato
- 1 cup light coconut milk
- 1 ½ lbs large shrimp, *peeled*
- ¾ cup broccoli, *chopped*

HOW TO MAKE

- Heat oil in skillet. Add onions and stir for 3 mins. Add garlic and ginger, cook 2 mins. Add spices and cook 1 min. Add tomatoes, broccoli, cook 2 mins. Add coconut milk, ½ cup water, and salt. Simmer until thickened 5-10 mins. Add shrimp, simmer 5 mins.

TUNA STUFFED *Avocado*

INGREDIENTS

For 4 servings

- 4 avocados, *halved*
- 4 cans (4.5 oz) tuna, *drained*
- ½ cup red onion, *diced*
- ½ cup cherry tomatoes, *halved*
- 1 tbsp lime juice

HOW TO MAKE

- Scoop out some of the avocado.
- Add the tuna, onion to the bowl. Pour lime juice. Stir together.
- Scoop the tuna into the avocado. Add tomatoes.

Dinner

One Pot SPICY QUINOA

INGREDIENTS

For 4 servings

- 1 onion, *sliced*
- 4 tbsp curry paste
- 4 cups almond milk
- 1½ cups frozen mixed vegetable
- 2 cups dry quinoa
- Avocado, *to serve*
- 1 can (15 oz) kidney beans

HOW TO MAKE

- Simmer the onion and the curry paste with a splash of water for 5 mins. Add the vegetables and quinoa, add salt to taste then stir in the milk. Bring to the boil, simmer gently for 10 mins until the quinoa is cooked.
- Serve with avocado, beans.

SALMON *Tartare*

INGREDIENTS

For 4 servings

- 1 tbsp olive oil
- 8 oz smoked salmon, *chopped*
- 2 spring onions, *chopped*
- 2 tbsp shallot, *chopped*
- 2 avocados, *chopped*

HOW TO MAKE

- Mix salmon with oil, shallots.
- Use measuring cup as a mold, and pack with the salmon mixture, top with avocado. Turn out onto plate. Garnish with spring onions.

TOMATO TUNA *Curry*

INGREDIENTS

For 4 servings

- 4 tuna steaks
- 1 tsp red chili powder
- 1 tsp ginger powder
- ½ tsp turmeric powder
- 3 red dried chilies, *halved*
- 2 tomatoes, *chopped*
- 1 onion, chopped
- 1 cup fish stock
- 1 tbsp olive oil

HOW TO MAKE

- Cut the tuna into medium chunks.
- Heat oil in saucepan. Add the onion and cook 1 min. Add the turmeric, chili powder, ginger powder, tomato, cook 6 mins. Pour in the fish stock. Bring it to boil. Add the fish, chili, and cook 15 mins.

BEAN BURRITO *Bowl*

INGREDIENTS

For 4 servings

- 2 (15oz) cans black beans
- 4 tbsp low fat cheese
- 1 can (15oz) corn kernels
- 4 tbsp tomato salsa
- 1 tsp ground cumin
- 1 tsp garlic powder
- 1½ cup brown rice

HOW TO MAKE

- Cook brown rice according to instructions.
- Drain and warm beans and corn.
- Serve rice with beans, corn, salsa, leftover chicken *(if you have)*, cheese.

CHICKPEA STUFFED *Kumara*

INGREDIENTS

For 4 servings

- 1 cup broccoli, *chopped*
- 1 medium bell pepper, *finely chopped*
- 4 medium kumara
- 1 can (15 oz) chickpeas, *drained*
- 1 tbsp olive oil

HOW TO MAKE

- Wash kumara thoroughly, pierce with a fork. Microwave 5 mins, turning halfway. Cut kumara in half and fluff their centers with a fork.
- Bake broccoli, bell pepper, chickpeas 15 mins at 375 °F.
- Spoon chickpeas into each kumara. Top with broccoli, bell pepper. Drizzle with oil.

BAKED SALMON *Balls*

Lunch

INGREDIENTS

For 4 servings

- 3 cans (6 oz) salmon
- 4 tbsp wholemeal breadcrumbs
- 2 scallion, *thinly sliced*
- 2 eggs, *lightly beaten*
- 2 tbsp fat-free greek yogurt
- 1 tbsp garlic, *minced*

HOW TO MAKE

- Preheat oven to 400°F.
- Combine all ingredients. Roll mixture into balls. Bake, flipping once, about 20 mins.

Dinner

CHICKEN & ARTICHOKE *Skillet*

INGREDIENTS

For 4 servings

- 4 chicken breasts
- Juice of 1 lemon
- 2 tbsp olive oil
- 3 cups marinated artichoke hearts
- ½ cup chicken broth
- Fresh parsley for garnish

HOW TO MAKE

- Cut chicken breasts into thin slices.
- Heat olive oil in a skillet. Add chicken, cook 6 mins.
- Pour lemon juice, chicken broth, artichoke hearts and simmer for 5 mins.

GREEK CHICKPEA *Salad*

INGREDIENTS

For 4 servings

- 1 can (15oz) chickpeas
- 2 cups cherry tomatoes
- ½ cup fresh basil
- ¼ cup onion, *slivered*
- 1 cup low fat feta cheese
- 2 tbsp olive oil
- 2 tbsp apple cider vinegar

HOW TO MAKE

- In a large bowl mix all vegetable and chickpeas.
- Drizzle with the olive oil and vinegar, season with salt to taste. Toss gently. Add feta cheese.

CURRY TURKEY *Stir-Fry*

INGREDIENTS

For 4 servings

- 1 lb turkey breast strips
- 1 medium carrot, *sliced*
- 2 cups cabbage, *chopped*
- 1 cup vegetable broth
- 2 tsp curry powder
- ½ tsp ground ginger

HOW TO MAKE

- Heat oil in skillet, Add turkey, salt to taste, cook 5 mins. Stir in carrot and cabbage. Cook 2 mins.
- In small bowl, mix remaining ingredients. Stir into turkey and vegetables. Heat to boiling, reduce heat. Cover and cook until turkey is no longer pink in center.

CAULIFLOWER *Taco Bowl*

INGREDIENTS

For 4 servings

- 6 cups cauliflower florets
- ½ cup sweet onion, *diced*
- 3 cloves garlic, *minced*
- 2 tbsp olive oil
- 1 tbsp chili powder
- 1 can (15oz) black beans

HOW TO MAKE

- Mix cauliflower, diced onion, olive oil, chili powder, and salt to taste.
- Preheat the oven to 400°F. Bake 20 mins. Serve with beans.

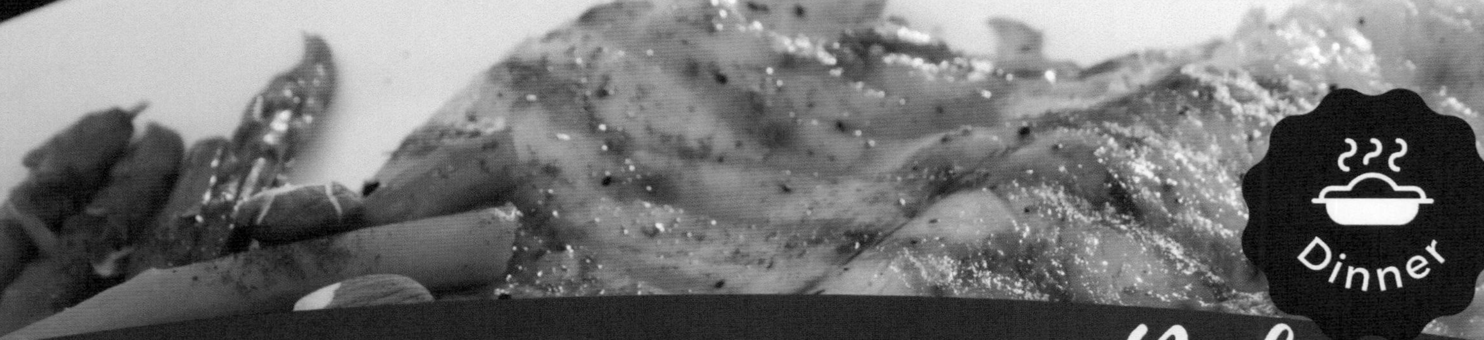

COD AND ASPARAGUS *Bake*

INGREDIENTS

For 4 servings

- 4 cod fillets (4 oz each)
- 1 lb thin asparagus, trimmed
- 2 cups cherry tomatoes, halved
- 2 tbsp lemon juice
- 1 tsp grated lemon zest
- ¼ cup reduced fat cheese, grated

HOW TO MAKE

- Place cod and asparagus in baking pan brushed with oil. Add tomatoes. Dizzle fish with lemon juice and sprinkle with lemon zest, salt to taste. Top with cheese.
- Preheat oven to 400°. Bake 15 mins.

MISO CHICKEN *Stir-fry*

Lunch

INGREDIENTS

For 4 servings

- 3 chicken breasts, *cut into bite size pieces*
- 2 tbsp olive oil
- 2 cloves garlic, *chopped*
- 2 bell peppers, *chopped*
- 2 tbsp yellow miso paste
- 1 tbsp coconut aminos

HOW TO MAKE

- Heat the oil in skillet. Add in the chicken pieces, cook 5 mins.
- Add garlic, peppers and cook 1 min. Add miso paste, coconut aminos and mix. Cook for 1-2 mins.

Dinner

PEPPER & KIDNEY BEAN *Stew*

INGREDIENTS

For 4 servings

- 1 can (15 oz) kidney beans, *drained*
- 1 can (11 oz) corn kernels, *drained*
- 1 can (15 oz) crushed tomatoes
- 1 tbsp olive oil
- 1 red onion, *diced*
- 1 tsp smoked paprika
- ½ tsp ground cinnamon
- 2 carrots, *chopped*
- 2 cups vegetable broth

HOW TO MAKE

- Heat the oil in skillet, add the onion and cook for 1 min. Add paprika, cook for 1 min. Stir in the carrots, broth, kidney beans and canned tomatoes.
- Simmer 15 mins. Add corn and cook 2 mins.

QUINOA *Soup*

INGREDIENTS

For 4 servings

- 2 tbsp olive oil
- 1 can (15 oz) cannellini beans
- 1 medium onion, *chopped*
- 1 large zucchini, *chopped*
- *8 cups vegetable broth*
- 2 carrots, *chopped*
- 1 cup quinoa

HOW TO MAKE

- Heat oil In a large pot. Add onion, carrot, salt to taste. Cook 5 mins.
- Add zucchini, beans, quinoa, cumin.
- Pour in broth and stir to combine.
- Bring to a boil and boil 15 mins.

Dinner

Sauteed BRUSSELS SPROUTS

INGREDIENTS

For 4 servings

- 2 tbsp olive oil
- 1 lb brussels sprouts
- 1 tbsp balsamic vinegar
- 1 tbsp english mustard
- 1 can (15 oz) lentils
- 1 tbsp olive oil
- ½ cup parsley

HOW TO MAKE

- Heat the oil in skillet, add brussels sprouts and cook 10 mins. Stir in lentils and remove from heat.
- Place brussels sprouts with lentils in a large bowl. Add balsamic vinegar, english mustard and chopped parsley, mix well to combine. Serve warm.

CASHEW THAI *Salad*

INGREDIENTS

For 4 servings

- ¼ cup lime juice
- 1 tbsp tamari
- 2 cups lettuce
- 2 tsp olive oil
- 2 cups carrot, finely shredded
- ¼ cup onion, thinly sliced
- 1½ cups roasted cashews

HOW TO MAKE

- In a large bowl mix all vegetables and cashews.
- Drizzle with the tamari, oil and lime juice. Toss gently.

Dinner

FAJITA CHICKEN *Traybake*

INGREDIENTS

For 4 servings

- 2 tbsp olive oil
- 2 red onions, sliced
- 2 tbsp fajita spice mix
- 3 mixed peppers, *sliced*
- 1 lb mini chicken fillets
- 1 can (15 oz) black beans, *drained*
- ½ cup fat-free greek yogurt
- 2 tbsp chopped coriander

HOW TO MAKE

- Preheat the oven to 400°F.
- In a large bowl, mix fajita spice, oil, onions, peppers and chicken. Tip into the hot baking sheet. Roast in the oven for 10 mins. Stir and cook for 5 mins.
- Mix in beans, bake for 5 mins.
- Serve with the greek yogurt and coriander.

KALE BEAN *Bowl*

INGREDIENTS

For 4 servings

- 1 clove garlic, *minced*
- 6 cups kale, *chopped*
- 2 cans (15oz) white beans
- ¼ cup walnuts, *chopped*
- ½ tbsp Italian seasoning
- 1 tbsp apple cider vinegar
- 1 tbsp olive oil

HOW TO MAKE

- Heat the oil in skillet, add kale and garlic. Sauté until the kale is wilted, Add bean and cook 1 min.
- Mix kale with the rest of ingredients serve warm

Dinner

LENTIL ZUCCHINI *Boats*

INGREDIENTS

For 4 servings

- 2 tbsp tamari
- 1 tbsp olive oil
- 1 medium onion, *chopped*
- 1 can (15 oz) lentils
- 4 medium zucchini
- ½ cup walnuts, *chopped*
- 1 can (15 oz) tomatoes
- ½ tsp Italian seasoning
- ½ cup low fat cheese, *grated*

HOW TO MAKE

- Cut the zucchini in half lengthwise, remove some of the flesh of the zucchini.
- Heat the oil in skillet. Fry onion, for a min. Add zucchini flesh, lentils, tamari, tomatoes, walnuts, spices. Cook 5 mins.
- Arrange lentil mixture in the zucchini boats, sprinkle with cheese, bake 10 mins at 400°F.

FISH *Tacos*

Lunch

INGREDIENTS

For 4 servings

- 1 lb fish fillets
- ½ cup fat-free greek yogurt
- 2 cups red cabbage, *shredded*
- 12 taco-sized corn tortillas
- 2 tomatoes, *thinly sliced*
- 4 radishes, *thinly sliced*
- 1 avocado, *sliced*

HOW TO MAKE

- Sprinkle the fish with salt. Add fish to the pan and cook for 2 mins. Flip fish and cook another 2 mins.
- Assemble the tacos with a few pieces of fish and other ingredients.

Dinner

MUSHROOM BUCKWHEAT *Risotto*

INGREDIENTS

For 4 servings

- 1½ cup buckwheat
- 16 oz mushrooms, *diced*
- 1 medium onion, *chopped*
- 1 cup green onions, *diced*
- 2 tbsp olive oil

HOW TO MAKE

- Cook buckwheat according to instructions on package.
- Heat the oil in skillet. Add onions and mushrooms cook until it becomes golden brown.
- Combine mushroom mixture with buckwheat, let it sit for about 5 mins to allow flavors to come together.

LENTIL TUNA *Salad*

Lunch

INGREDIENTS

For 4 servings

- 1 tbsp apple cider vinegar
- 1 tsp Dijon mustard
- 2 garlic cloves, *minced*
- 2 tbsp olive oil
- 1 (15 oz) can lentils, *drained*
- 2 (6 oz) cans tuna, *drained*
- 2 bell peppers, *chopped*

HOW TO MAKE

- Whisk the vinegar, mustard, oil, garlic together.
- Add the lentils, tuna, peppers to a large bowl and toss together. Pour over the dressing and toss again.

Dinner

TOFU TERIYAKI *Bowl*

INGREDIENTS

For 4 servings

- 14 oz. firm tofu, *cut in cubes*
- 1 tsp ginger, *freshly grated*
- 1 medium onion, *sliced*
- 2 spring onions, *chopped*
- 3 tsp Monk fruit sweetener
- 2 cups brown rice
- 2 tbsp olive oil
- 2 tbsp tamari

HOW TO MAKE

- Cook rice according to instructions on package.
- Heat the oil in skillet. Add tofu to the pan, fry 5 mins.
- Add the ginger, onions, tamari, sweetener. Stir-fry for 2-3 mins.
- Serve over rice with spring onions

SALMON *Rolls*

INGREDIENTS

For 4 servings

- 8 large slices smoked salmon
- 1 cup low fat cream cheese
- 2 tbsp horseradish
- 1 tbsp lemon juice
- ½ cup cucumber sticks
- ½ cup carrot sticks

HOW TO MAKE

- Whisk cream cheese with horseradish, lemon juice.
- Spread cream cheese mixture onto salmon slices and top with cucumber and carrot sticks. Roll up.

Salsa BAKED FISH

INGREDIENTS

For 4 servings

- 1 cup barley
- 1 tbsp olive oil
- 1 lb white fish
- 1 cup salsa
- 1 small zucchini, *diced*
- 2 bell peppers
- 1 cup tomatoes, *chopped*
- 2 garlic cloves, *minced*
- ½ lemon

HOW TO MAKE

- Cook barley according to instructions on package.
- Place all vegetables into a bowl, drizzle in enough olive oil, salt and pepper to taste.
- Generously top the filets with the salsa, add in a few lemon wedges. Place vegetables around. Bake 15 mins at 400°F.
- Serve with barley.

AVOCADO EGG *Sandwiches*

INGREDIENTS

For 4 servings

- Juice 1 lime
- 8 slices rye bread
- 4 boiled eggs
- 2 ripe avocados
- 4 tsp hot sriracha
- Handful cress, to serve

HOW TO MAKE

- Spread the avocado on bread. Cut the eggs in half and place on top of the avocado.
- Drizzle some chilli sauce over the eggs, top with cress.

Stuffed MUSHROOMS

INGREDIENTS

For 4 servings

- 2 cups quinoa
- ½ cup wholemeal breadcrumbs
- ½ cup low fat cheese, *grated*
- 2 garlic cloves, *minced*
- 2 tbsp parsley, *chopped*
- 1 tbsp olive oil
- 12 large portobello mushroom caps

HOW TO MAKE

- Cook quinoa according to instructions on package.
- Stir the breadcrumbs, cheese, garlic, parsley, salt to taste, olive oil together.
- Spoon the filling into the mushroom and arrange on the baking sheet.
- Bake 25 mins at 400°F.
- Serve with quinoa.

BULGUR *Bean Salad*

INGREDIENTS

For 4 servings

- 1 cup bulgur
- 1 cup shelled edamame
- 1 cup sun-dried tomatoes
- 1 cup basil, *chopped*
- ½ cup green onions, *chopped*
- ¼ cup lemon juice
- 2 tbsp olive oil

HOW TO MAKE

- Cook bulgur according to instructions on package.
- Cook edamame in boiling water 3 mins. Drain.
- Add all ingredient to bulgur, mix.

Dinner

SWEET POTATO & BEAN *Skillet*

INGREDIENTS

For 4 servings

- 1 tbsp olive oil
- 2 cups sweet potato, *diced*
- 1 ½ tsp chili powder
- 1 tsp ground cumin
- 1 tsp dried oregano
- ½ tsp smoked paprika
- 4 oz green chiles, *diced*
- ½ cup salsa
- 1 (15 oz) can black beans

HOW TO MAKE

- Heat oil in a skillet. Add potatoes, salt to taste, sauté over medium heat 10 mins. Add 4 tbsp of water and cover it with a lid. Let the sweet potatoes steam 4 mins.
- Add remain ingredients. Stir everything together. Cover the skillet with lid. Cook for another 4 mins.

CREAMY CARROT *Bean Soup*

INGREDIENTS

For 4 servings

- 2 tbsp olive oil
- 1 clove garlic, *minced*
- 1 red onion, *diced*
- 4 cups vegetable stock
- 2 cups carrots, *cut into coins*
- 1 (15 oz) can cannellini beans

HOW TO MAKE

- Add the oil to a pot. Add the garlic, onion and cook 2 mins.
- Add the vegetable stock, carrots, beans (drained). Cook 15 mins.
- Puree with blender, add salt to taste

CRAB & MUSHROOM *Zoodles*

INGREDIENTS

For 4 servings

- 2 cups jumbo lump crab meat
- 1 cup mushrooms, *chopped*
- 4 zucchinis, *peeled, noodles trimmed*
- 1 garlic clove, *minced*
- 2 tsp olive oil
- 1 avocado
- 1 lime juiced

HOW TO MAKE

- Heat olive oil in a skillet. Add the mushrooms, salt to taste. Cook 7 mins.
- Blend avocado, garlic, lime juice in a blender until creamy.
- Place the zucchini noodles into a bowl, add avocado sauce, toss until combined. Add the crab, mushrooms and toss again.

HUMMUS *Bowl*

INGREDIENTS

For 4 servings

- 2 avocados, *sliced*
- 2 cups carrot sticks
- 2 cups red cabbage, *shredded*
- 1 tbsp lemon juice
- 2 tbsp tahini
- 2 garlic cloves
- 1 tbsp olive oil

HOW TO MAKE

- Bend until creamy: lemon juice, garlic, chickpeas, oil, tahini, salt.
- Spoon the hummus onto a bowl.
- Assemble the remaining ingredients on top of the hummus.

Dinner

Shrimp BRUSSELS SPROUTS

INGREDIENTS

For 4 servings

- 1 tbsp apple cider vinegar
- 1 tbsp tamari
- 2 tsp ginger, *grated*
- 1 lb shrimp, *peeled*
- 2 tbsp olive oil
- 1 lb brussels sprouts, *trimmed*
- 3 cloves garlic, *thinly sliced*
- 1 red onion, *sliced*

HOW TO MAKE

- Whisk together vinegar, tamari and ginger. Add shrimp and toss to combine. Let it sit 10 mins.
- Preheat oven to 400°F. Place the shrimp on baking sheet in the center.
- Surround the shrimp with brussels sprouts, onion. Bake for 10-15 mins.

OATMEAL PANCAKES

For 4 servings

- 2⅓ cups oat flour
- 3 tbsp flaxseed meal
- 2 tsp baking powder
- 2 cups almond milk
- 1 tsp olive oil

Blend all ingredient, salt to taste in blender to make batter. In a skillet set over medium heat, brush some oil. Pour batter, fry until you see bubbles form. Then flip and fry on the other side until golden brown.

QUINOA CEREAL

For 4 servings

- 4 cups almond milk
- 2 cups rinsed quinoa
- 2 tsp Monk fruit sweetener
- Pinch of ground cinnamon
- ½ cup fat-free greek yogurt
- Fresh berries

Bring milk and quinoa to a boil in saucepan. Simmer, covered, about 14 mins. Remove from heat and stir in sweetener, cinnamon. Top with yogurt and berries.

SPINACH EGG MUFFINS

For 4 servings

- ½ cup dried tomatoes, *sliced*
- 1 cup spinach, *finely diced*
- ½ onion, *finely diced*
- 8 large eggs
- ¼ cup almond milk
- ⅓ cup low fat feta cheese crumbles

Preheat oven to 400°F. Process milk, eggs, spinach, salt and pepper to taste in food processor. Pour the egg mixture into the muffin tin. Add in tomatoes, onions. Bake 20 mins.

FLAXSEED OATMEAL

For 4 servings

- 2 cups almond milk
- 2 cup rolled oats
- 4 tbsp walnuts, *chopped*
- 2 tsp Monk fruit sweetener
- 1 cup fresh blueberries
- 4 tbsp flaxseed meal
- 2 apples

In a saucepan bring milk and water (1 ½ cup) to a boil. Reduce the heat to medium-low and stir in oats, flaxseed, and salt. Cook for 6-7 mins, uncovered. Serve with apple and walnuts.

BUCKWHEAT PANCAKES

For 4 servings

- 1 cup buckwheat flour
- 2 tsp Monk fruit sweetener
- 2 tsp baking soda
- ⅛ tsp salt
- 1 ¼ cups almond milk
- 2 eggs

Blend all ingredient in blender to make batter. In a skillet set over medium heat, brush some oil. Pour batter, fry until you see bubbles form. Flip and fry on the other side until golden brown.

CHIA WAFFLES

For 4 servings

- 1 ¾ cups almond milk
- ½ cup applesauce
- 1 egg, *beaten*
- 2 tsp chia seeds
- ½ cup whole wheat flour
- 1 ¼ cups rolled oats
- ¼ cup flaxseed meal
- 4 tsp baking powder
- 1 tbsp Monk fruit sweetener

Blend all ingredient in blender. Scoop ½ cup batter into the preheated waffle iron and cook about 5 mins per waffle.

CRISPY CAULIFLOWER

INGREDIENTS:

For 4 servings

- 1 medium head of cauliflower
- 2 tbsp olive oil
- 1 tsp garlic powder
- ½ tsp smoked paprika
- ½ tsp turmeric powder

HOW TO MAKE:

Cut the cauliflower into florets.
In a large bowl, add the florets, spices, salt and pepper to taste, olive oil and toss the florets so the spices are evenly coated.
Preheat Air fryer at 380°F for 5 mins.
Place cauliflower in a single layer in Air fryer basket. Cook 10 mins.

ZUCCHINI FRIES

INGREDIENTS:

For 4 servings

- 2 zucchinis cut into fries
- ⅔ cup almond flour
- ¼ cup low fat cheese
- 1 tsp smoked paprika
- Olive oil spray

HOW TO MAKE:

- Combine almond flour, cheese, paprika, salt to taste in a bowl.
- Spray zucchini with olive oil.
- Dip zucchini fries into the cheese mixture.
- Preheat Air fryer at 400°F for 5 mins. Place fries in a single layer. Cook 7-10 mins.

Air Fryer BANANA BREAD

INGREDIENTS

For 4 servings

- 1 ⅓ cups whole wheat flour
- ½ cups almond milk
- 1 tsp baking powder
- 1 tsp baking soda
- 1 tsp cinnamon
- ½ cup of olive oil
- 6 overripe bananas

HOW TO MAKE

- Mix together all of the ingredients in a mixer.
- Then spray your pan with non-stick cooking spray
- Cook in the Air Fryer at 400°F for 20-25 mins.

Printed in Great Britain
by Amazon